SCIENCE in Action

KEEPING HEALTHY

Why do I brush my teeth?

Angela Royston

Quarto is the authority on a wide range of topics.

Quarto educates, entertains and enriches the lives of our readers—enthusiasts and lovers of hands-on living.

www.quartoknows.com

First published in the UK in 2016 by
QED Publishing
Part of The Quarto Group
The Old Brewery, 6 Blundell Street,
London, N7 9BH

A catalogue record for this book is available from the British Library.

ISBN 978 1 78493 629 7

Printed and bound in China

Publisher: Maxime Boucknooghe
Editorial Director: Victoria Garrard
Art Director: Miranda Snow
Design and Editorial: Starry Dog Books Ltd
Consultant: Kristina Routh

Picture credits
(t=top, b=bottom, l=left, r=right, c=centre, fc=front cover)
Corbis Barbara Peacock 7b
Getty Images ERproductions Ltd fc, Karen Moskowitz 5t, Joe Major 21b
Shutterstock Jacek Chabraszewski 4, Igor Kisselev 5b, Flashon Studio 6, Pixel Memoirs 7t, Vinicius Tupinamba 8, alphabe 9t, mikeledray 9b, James Steidl 11t, Kunertus 11b, Patrick Foto 12, Vlas2000 13t, Alexeysun 13b, Larisa Lofitskaya 14l, Pavel Sazonov 14r, Larisa Lofitskaya 15l, Rob Byron 15r, Nobor 16c, Galushko Sergey 16bl, Nuno Garuti 16br, Sergey Peterman 16cr, Ismael Montero Verdu 16cl, Scott Rothstein 17t, Stuart Monk 17b, Chiyacat 18bl, Sandra Caldwell 18cl, Skazka Grez 18cr, Birgit Reitz-Hofmann 18r, Sergieiev 19l, Cen 19c, Andrey Armyagov 19tr, gorillaimages 19b, Dmitriy Shironosov 20, David J Morgan 21b.

Words in **bold** can be found in the glossary on page 22.

Contents

Why do I have teeth?

Teeth are what we use to bite into our food. We also chew food with our teeth so that we can swallow it easily. Brushing teeth regularly keeps our teeth clean and strong.

Strong teeth can bite through tough foods, such as crusty bread.

Activity

Use a mirror to check your teeth. How many teeth do you have? Do you have any gaps?

We also use our teeth when we speak – especially our front teeth. Try saying the word 'teeth' without touching your front teeth with your tongue.

Your teeth help you to make the sounds 'f' and 'th'.

5

Two sets of teeth

We have two sets of teeth in our lifetime. Our first teeth are called baby teeth, or milk teeth. They begin to appear when we are about six to nine months old. By the time we are five, we will have 20 teeth.

This baby has two teeth. Our first teeth are usually on the bottom jaw.

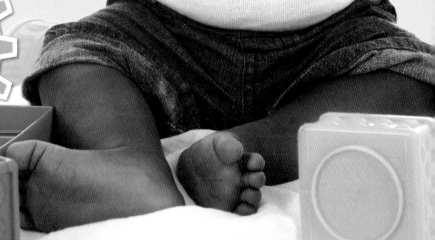

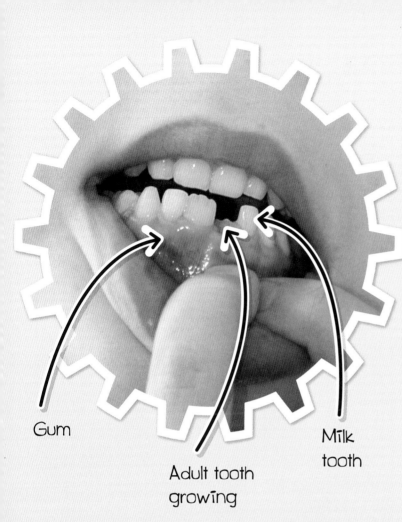

Gum

Adult tooth growing

Milk tooth

Our second set of teeth are called permanent or adult teeth. They start off inside our gums, where we can't see them. As they grow bigger, they push out our milk teeth. We have 32 adult teeth.

Activity

Next time one of your milk teeth falls out, look at it closely. Can you see any root? Compare its size to an adult tooth.

Types of teeth

We have three types of teeth. Our front teeth have a wide, sharp edge, and are called incisors. We use them like a knife to slice through food.

Our front teeth are sharp enough to bite into a crunchy apple.

8

Next to our front teeth are our pointed canine teeth. We use these to tear off pieces of food.

At the backs of our mouths are some larger, flatter teeth called molars. These are used for chewing.

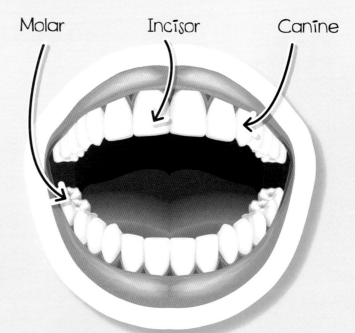

Molar   Incisor   Canine

Our different-shaped teeth do different jobs, such as biting or chewing.

Activity

Take a bite from a fruit, such as a pear. Now try chewing it using just your front teeth. Is it easier or more difficult than using your back teeth?

9

Inside a tooth

A tooth has three layers. In the centre is a core of soft **pulp**. It contains blood vessels and nerves. The middle layer is called **dentine**. It's as strong as bone. The outer layer is made of **enamel**, and it's the hardest thing in your body!

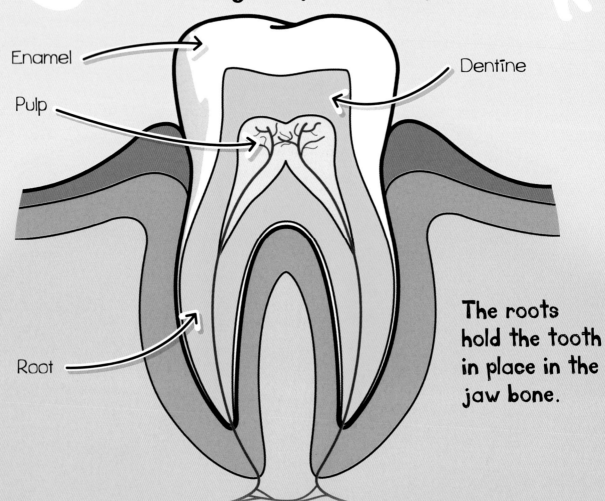

Enamel

Dentine

Pulp

Root

The roots hold the tooth in place in the jaw bone.

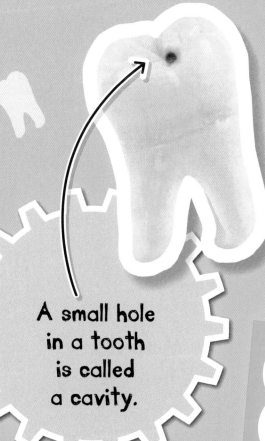

Acid can damage our teeth by making the hard layer of enamel go soft. This is called **tooth decay**. It can make holes in our teeth.

A small hole in a tooth is called a cavity.

Activity

Put an uncooked egg into a glass, cover it with vinegar and leave it overnight. Vinegar is an acid. It takes the **calcium** out of the eggshell in the same way that acid in your mouth attacks your teeth. In the morning, the eggshell will be soft.

Causes of tooth decay

Each day, a very thin, sticky layer builds up on our teeth. This layer is called **plaque**. It contains millions of tiny germs called bacteria.

The bacteria feed on sugar in our mouths, and produce acid. If we don't brush the acid off, it can cause tooth decay.

A hole in a tooth can be very painful.

Dentists can treat tooth decay. They drill away the rotten part of the tooth and fill the hole. This is called having a filling.

When a dentist fills a tooth, it stops decaying.

Eye

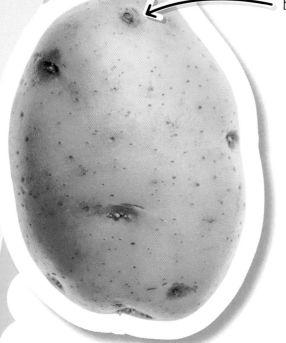

Activity

Be a dentist! Find a large potato with 'eyes' in it. With adult help, dig out the eyes with a potato peeler. Put a teaspoon of flour into a bowl and add a few drops of water. Fill the holes with the mixture, just as a dentist fills teeth!

Cleaning your teeth

Brushing teeth gets rid of the sugar and plaque that can cause tooth decay. That's why it's important that we brush our teeth in the morning and at bedtime.

Try to clean your teeth after eating anything sweet.

We should brush all the surfaces of each tooth. This means brushing the backs as well as the fronts, and along the tops of our molars. Brush for two minutes, twice a day.

Activity

Once in a while, check how well you are brushing your teeth. Brush them as normal, then chew a disclosing tablet. This will dye any remaining plaque red or purple. Then brush your teeth again!

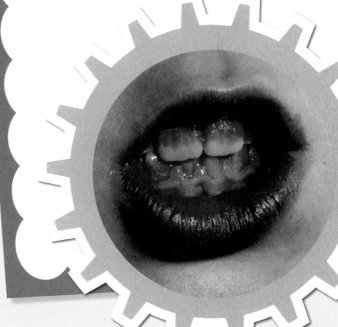

Sugar damages teeth

Fizzy drinks and foods such as biscuits, sweets, doughnuts and cakes all contain lots of sugar. When we eat them, some of the sugar stays in our mouths and can cause tooth decay.

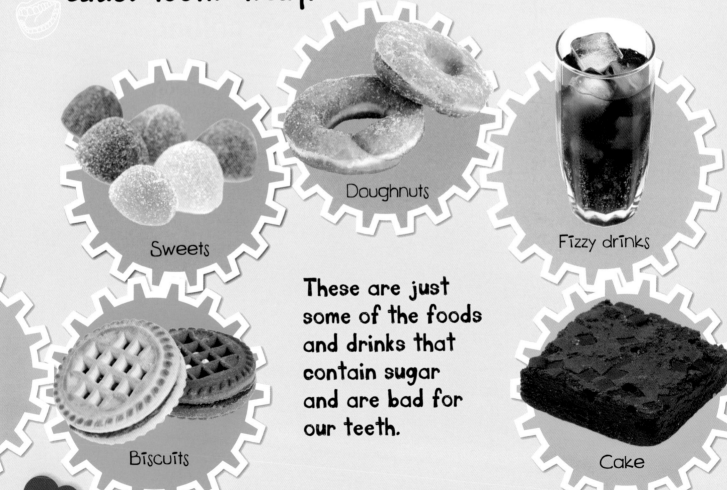

Doughnuts

Fizzy drinks

Sweets

These are just some of the foods and drinks that contain sugar and are bad for our teeth.

Biscuits

Cake

Activity

After using your toothbrush, wash it well in clean water. Examine it carefully to make sure all the bits of food have been washed away.

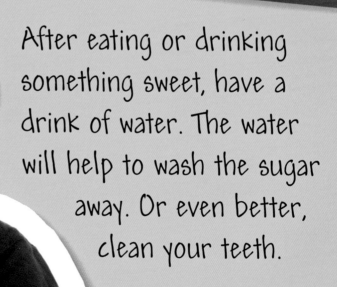

After eating or drinking something sweet, have a drink of water. The water will help to wash the sugar away. Or even better, clean your teeth.

Drinking water helps to clean our teeth.

17

Making teeth stronger

Our teeth are strong because they contain a mineral called calcium. We can make them even stronger by eating foods that contain calcium. Strong teeth are less likely to get holes in them.

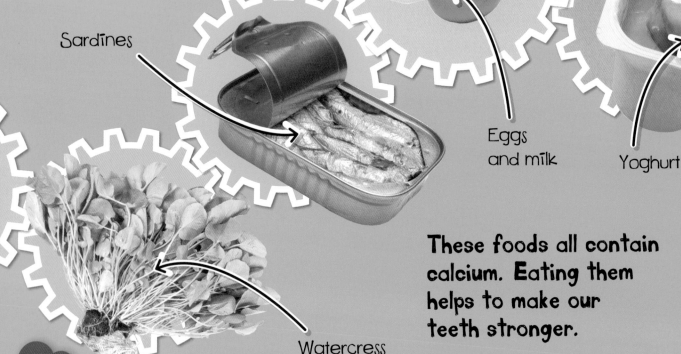

Sardines

Eggs and milk

Yoghurt

Watercress

These foods all contain calcium. Eating them helps to make our teeth stronger.

Most types of toothpaste contain a substance called **fluoride**. This makes the enamel on our teeth stronger. In some places, fluoride is added to tap water.

Bread

Cheese

Try not to swallow toothpaste. If we often have too much fluoride, it can stain our teeth brown.

Activity

Make a healthy, calcium-filled lunch. You could start with a cheese and salad sandwich. Then you could eat a yoghurt or an orange.

19

Visiting the dentist

We should visit the dentist every six months for a check-up. Dentists look at all our teeth to see if we have any tooth decay. They also check our adult teeth to make sure they are growing well.

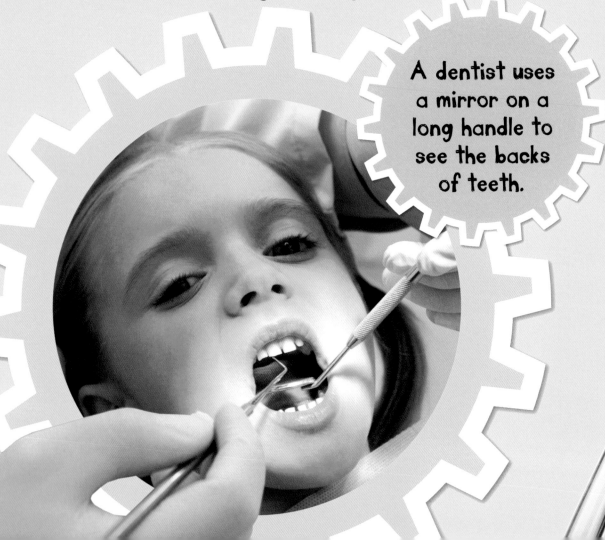

A dentist uses a mirror on a long handle to see the backs of teeth.

Sometimes we get toothache. Eating something very cold can give us a sharp pain in a tooth. Usually the pain goes away quickly, but if it stays, visit a dentist.

Ice cream can make our teeth hurt, but usually just for a moment.

New

Activity

Old

Check your toothbrush to make sure the bristles are straight and firm. If they are not, you need a new toothbrush.

21

Glossary

Calcium
The substance that makes our teeth and bones hard and strong.

Dentine
The main part of a tooth is made of dentine. It is similar to bone and is covered with a layer of very hard enamel.

Enamel
The hard, glossy, outer layer of a tooth. Enamel contains calcium and fluoride.

Fluoride
One of the substances that makes the enamel and dentine in our teeth strong. Most toothpastes contain fluoride.

Plaque
A sticky substance in our mouths that contains bacteria. Acid in the plaque can cause tooth decay. Cleaning our teeth helps to remove plaque and stop it forming.

Pulp
This is the soft material in the centre of a tooth. It contains blood vessels and nerves.

Tooth decay
Tooth decay begins when acid in the mouth eats a hole in the enamel of a tooth. If the decay spreads to the soft pulp in the centre of the tooth where the nerves are, it can be very painful.

Index

NEXT STEPS

❀ Search the Internet to find diagrams of a full set of milk teeth and a full set of permanent teeth. Count the teeth and see which extra teeth are included in the permanent teeth. Copy the plans of the teeth and help your child to colour in the milk teeth that they have already lost, and the permanent teeth that have already come through. Some families leave money from the 'Tooth Fairy' under a child's pillow whenever a milk tooth falls out.

❀ Talk about tooth decay and the foods that contribute to it. Make a list of drinks and foods, particularly snacks, that contain a lot of refined sugar. Discuss how you can limit the intake of these foods to once or twice a day, and how drinking water after eating them – or, better still, brushing teeth – helps to prevent tooth decay.

❀ Talk to your child about the importance of brushing teeth twice a day for two minutes. Explain how this will help to prevent tooth decay.

❀ Brush your teeth, then demonstrate how to use a disclosing tablet. Enourage the children to have a go. Compare results – who cleaned their teeth best? Explain to the children that they should only use disclosing tablets occasionally.

❀ Take your child for a dental check-up every six months. Set an example by having your own teeth checked at the same time.